Christmas Jokes For Kids

Giggles All The Way For Little Elves To Enjoy And Have Fun | Kids Joke Book Ages 7-12

Amina Poole

Contents

"A day without LAUGHTER is a day WASTED."

Charles Chaplin

Introduction

Christmas is a time of heartwarming joy, cherished family reunions, and age-old customs. The air fills with the fragrance of pine trees and freshly baked cookies, accompanied by the gleeful laughter of children unwrapping gifts in their festive attire. What could infuse more merriment into this holiday season than a hearty chuckle?

Introducing our side-splitting Christmas joke book for kids! Overflowing with "ho-ho-hilarious" jokes, this compilation is crafted to enchant young minds and leave them in fits of laughter. Whether they're just starting to read or already proficient in delivering a punchline, our Christmas-themed quips will keep them entertained for hours.

In a world that often feels overwhelmingly serious, we believe that laughter and fun are essential for children's well-being. That's why we've crafted this Christmas joke book to inject a dose of humor into your family's holiday festivities. So gather your little elves and reindeer around and prepare to giggle because when it comes to tickling funny bones, not even Santa Claus can outdo us!

The essence of our Christmas joke book is the timeless delight of spending precious moments with those who matter most to us. These cherished connections form the basis for lifelong bonds, and what better way to strengthen them than through laughter? So, whether you're planning a holiday gathering, partaking in a festive parade, or simply seeking some seasonal fun at home, our jokes add the perfect touch of whimsy to create enduring memories.

With our Christmas joke book, your celebrations will be filled with laughter and unforgettable moments. Whether you're hosting a festive party, embarking on a gift-giving adventure, or just enjoying a cozy evening at home, our jokes provide a jolly way to infuse merriment into the festivities.

So, let's deck the halls and get ready for a joyous good time!

1.
Santa Claus
Jokes

What do you call when Santa takes his break?

Santa Pause!

Why does Santa always carry a red pen?

To draw his "claus" in every situation!

What's Santa's favorite candy?

Jolly Ranchers!

Why did Santa start a detective agency?

Because he loved "sleigh"-ing it!

Why did Santa go to space?

To find the Milky Way and share it with the reindeer!

What's Santa's favorite kind of pizza?

One that's deep-pan, crisp, and even!

Why does Santa like to work in his garden?

Because he has a "green thumb"!

Why did Santa bring a ladder to the Christmas party?

Because he heard the drinks were on the house!

Why was Santa's little helper feeling sad?

Because he had low "elf"-esteem!

What do you get when you cross Santa with a detective?

Santa Clues!

Why was Santa's math book so sad?

Because it had too many problems.

What did Santa say to the smoker?

Please don't smoke; it's bad for my "chimney"!

How does Santa keep his suits wrinkle-free?

He uses Claus-tarch!

Why was Santa's computer on the naughty list?

Because it had too many "ho ho ho"-rror messages!

What do you call Santa when he takes a nap?

Santa Snooze!

What do you call Santa when he loses his pants?

Saint Knickerless!

How does Santa keep track of all the presents he delivers?

He uses an "elf"-abetical system!

Why did Santa go to music school?

Because he wanted to improve his "wrap" skills!

Why did Santa bring a ladder to Christmas?

He heard the presents were stacked!

Where does Santa stay when he goes on a vacation?

At a ho-ho-ho-tel.

What do you call Santa when he takes a selfie?

Santa Snap!

Why did Santa go to the doctor?

Because he was "Claus"-trophobic in chimneys!

Why does Santa Claus wear a red suit?

Because it's Claus for celebration!

Why did Santa bring a ladder to the North Pole?

Because he heard the penguins were playing hide and seek on the icebergs!

What does Santa say when he's telling a joke?

"Ho-ho-ho-kay, here's a good one!"

What do you call Santa when he takes a nap in the workshop?

Santa Snore-a-lot!

Why did Santa put his money in the blender?

Because he wanted
to make some "jolly" bills!

Why did Santa take his sleigh to the auto shop?

It had a "snow-mobile" problem!

What do you get if you cross Santa with a kangaroo?

Santa Paws!

What do you call Santa when he loses his way on Christmas Eve?

Lost Claus!

Why did Santa go to the beach during Christmas?

He wanted to catch some "sandy claws"!

What kind of car does Santa drive on Christmas Eve?

A "Claustrover"!

What's Santa's favorite type of music?

Wrap music!

What does Santa use to repair his sleigh?

An "icicle" tape!

Do you know the kid who was scared of Santa?

He was Claus-trophobic!

Why did Santa wear a helmet while delivering presents?

To make sure he had a "sleigh"-ride without accidents!

Why did Santa bring a broom to the North Pole?

Because he wanted to "sweep" away the snow!

Why did Santa bring a calendar to Christmas?

Because he wanted to check his "dates" twice!

Why was Santa's computer cold?

It left its Windows open!

What did Santa say at the start of the race?

Ready, set, ho ho ho!

What does Santa do when the reindeer drive too fast?

Hold on for deer life.

What do you get when you cross Santa with a detective and a baker?

Santa Clues, who solves the mystery of the missing cookies!

Who's Santa Claus's favorite pop star?

It's Beyon-sleigh.

What do you call a bankrupt Santa?

Saint Nick-el-less.

2.
Christmas Tree
Jokes

What do you call a Christmas tree with no decorations?

Pine and simple!

What do Christmas trees use to communicate during the holidays?

Tree-phones!

Why did the Christmas tree go to the barber?

Because it needed a trim-tastic new look!

What's a tree's favorite classic movie during the holidays?

"Pine Alone"!

What do you call a Christmas tree that tells jokes?

A "punny" tree!

How do Christmas trees knit sweaters?

With "purl" needles and "yarn" ornaments!

What do you call a snowman hanging out with a Christmas tree?

Frosty and "tree-mendous" company!

How do Christmas trees keep in touch with each other?

They use "pine"-terest!

Why did the Christmas tree bring a ladder to the holiday party?

It wanted to "branch" out and
meet new friends!

What did one Christmas tree say to the other?

"I'm pining for you!"

How do Christmas trees get on the internet?

They log in!

Why was the Christmas tree so bad at knitting?

It kept dropping its needles!

How do Christmas trees stay cool during the holidays?

They use tree fans!

Why did the Christmas tree bring an extension cord to the party?

It wanted to "lighten up" the atmosphere!

What did one Christmas ornament say to the other?

"I like hanging out with you!"

Why do Christmas trees make terrible poker players?

They're always "green" and give away their hand!

What do you call a group of musical Christmas trees?

A "tree"-o!

What do you get when you cross a Christmas tree with an iPhone?

A pineapple!

What did the Christmas tree say to the ornament?

"You really bring out the 'tree'mendous in me!"

Why was the Christmas tree always good at shopping?

Because it had lots of branches to reach for the top deals!

Why did the Christmas tree want to be a rock star?

Because it wanted to be "tree-mendously" popular!

3.

Reindeer Jokes

Why did Rudolph get a bad report card?

Because he went down in history!

What's a reindeer's favorite dessert?

Ice-cream!

What do you call a reindeer who tells jokes?

A "comedi-deer"!

Why don't reindeer go to the movies?

Because they'd rather watch the "snow-flicks"!

What did the reindeer say before telling a joke?

"This will sleigh you!"

What do reindeer hang on their Christmas trees?

Horn-aments!

Why do reindeer tell the best stories?

Because they sleigh the competition!

How do you know if a reindeer is telling you a joke?

You'll hear the "bells" ringing!

Why did the reindeer start a podcast?

He had a lot of "deer" friends to interview!

What do you call a reindeer with no eyes?

No-eye-deer!

Why don't reindeer play cards in the wild?

Because there are too many cheetahs!

What's a reindeer's favorite game at the North Pole?

"Freeze and Seek"!

Why did the reindeer bring a ladder to the Christmas party?

Because it wanted to get on the "rooftop"!

What do you call a reindeer that tells stories?

A "tail"-teller!

How do you know if a reindeer is telling a secret?

It says, "Shhh-anta told me!"

Why did the reindeer apply for a job at the post office?

It wanted to be an "express" delivery reindeer!

What do you call a reindeer with no manners?

"Rude"-olph!

What do you call a reindeer that tells you the weather forecast?

A "rain"-deer!

Why don't reindeer
ever get lost?

They always "sleigh" it with their GPS!

What's a reindeer's
favorite candy?

Jingle "bells"!

Why did the reindeer bring a pencil
to the Christmas party?

In case it had to "draw" some attention!

Why did the reindeer apply for a job at the bakery?

Because it wanted to be a "dough"-deer!

What do you get when you cross a reindeer and a snake?

"Frost"-bite!

What's a reindeer's favorite type of music?

"Wrap" music!

What do you get when you cross a reindeer with an astronaut?

"Star"-dancer!

What's a reindeer's favorite fast food?

"Deer"ios!

What do the reindeer say to Santa on Christmas Eve?

We are ready to sleigh.

What kind of money do reindeer?

Bucks!

Where does the reindeer stop for coffee?

Star-bucks!

How did the reindeer know it was going to rain?

Because Rudolph the red-knows-rain, deer!

What's a reindeer's favorite TV show?

"Hoof"-ball games!

What do you call a reindeer that loves to read books?

A "read"-deer!

What did the reindeer say to the snowman?

"You're cool, but I'm cooler!"

4.
Gingerbread
Jokes

Why did the gingerbread cookie go to the doctor?

Because it was feeling crumby!

What's Santa's favorite type of cookie?

"Santa-mental" chocolate chip!

What did one gingerbread cookie say to the other?

"You're sweet enough to make my holiday complete!"

What do you call a gingerbread man with one leg bitten off?

A "half-baked" cookie!

How do gingerbread people celebrate birthdays?

With lots of "cookie-cake"!

How do you make a gingerbread house?

With "icing" and "cand-everything"!

How do gingerbread people keep their homes safe?

They have "cookie-curity"!

Why was the chef so good at making gingerbread?

Because they had "elf"-esteem!

What do gingerbread people do when they feel stressed?

They practice "cookie-cise" to relax!

How do gingerbread people start their day?

With a "cookie-cup" of coffee!

Why did the gingerbread cookie go to therapy?

Because it felt crumbled inside!

Why did the gingerbread person bring a book to the cookie party?

Because it wanted to have a "sweet" read!

Why did the gingerbread man start a band?

Because he had a "sweet" sound!

What does the gingerbread man put on his bed?

The Cookie sheets.

5.

Snowman

Jokes

Why did the snowman bring a scarf to the bar?

Because it wanted to get "chilled" to the bone!

What do snowmen wear on their heads?

Ice caps!

What did the snowman say to the aggressive carrot?

"Get out of my face; I've got my eyes on you!"

Why does the snowman look through the carrots?

He is picking his nose!

What's a snowman's favorite breakfast cereal?

Frosted Flakes!

How do snowmen travel around?

By riding an "icicle"!

How do snowmen stay warm in winter?

They use "flurry" blankets!

What did one snowman say to the other snowman?

"Hey, do you wanna build a snowman?"

Why was the snowman so good at math?

Because he had lots of "snow"-lutions!

What's a snowman's favorite relative?

Aunt Arctica!

Why did the snowman call his dog Frost?

Because Frost bites!

What do snowmen like to do on the weekend?

Chill out!

What do you call a snowman with a sunburn?

A puddle!

Why did the snowman bring a broom to the snowstorm?

He wanted to clean up his act!

How do you know if a snowman is a morning person?

He's up with the crack of dawn!

How do you make a snowstorm really angry?

Tell it to flake off!

What do you call a snowman with a six pack?

An abdominal snowman!

Why did the snowman call his friend on the phone?

He wanted to have a "chill" chat!

How do snowmen communicate during the holidays?

They use "snow"-signals!

Why was the snowman looking through the calendar?

He wanted to see his "cool" dates!

How do you make a snowman disappear?

Give him a warm hug!

What do snowmen call their sons and daughters?

Chill-dren.

What is the snowman's favorite type of food?

The Iceberg-ers!

What do snowmen take when the sun gets too hot?

A chill pill.

What song do you sing at a snowman's birthday party?

Freeze a jolly good fellow!

Where would you find a snowman dancing?

At a snowball!

What's a snowman's favorite kind of dance?

The "snowball"!

6.
Gifts Jokes

Why did the gift go to school?

Because it wanted to get a little "present"-ation!

Why did the present blush?

Because it saw the gift tag!

Why did the gift run a marathon?

It wanted to be a "long-lasting" surprise!

What do you get when you cross a gift with a phone?

A present call!

Why did the gift bring a ladder to the party?

It wanted to take the celebration to new heights!

What did the gift say to the birthday cake?

"I'm all wrapped up in you!"

What's a gift's favorite game to play?

"Wrap, Paper, Scissors"!

Why was the gift always happy?

Because it was good at "presents"!

Why did the gift bring a map to the party?

It wanted to find its way to the heart!

How do gifts stay cool during the summer?

They "wrap" themselves in shade!

What do you call a gift that loves to tell stories?

A "gift"-ed storyteller!

What did one gift say to the other gift?

"You're "wrap"-tivating!"

What's a gift's favorite type of puzzle?

A "wrapped" one!

What do you get if you cross a gift and a bicycle?

A present with too many "wheels"!

Why was the gift always so polite?

Because it had "present"-able manners!

Why did the computer go shopping for presents?

Because it wanted to buy some byte-sized gifts!

Why is a foot a good Christmas gift?

It fits right in a stocking.

Why don't presents ever play hide and seek?

Because they're always good at being wrapped up!

How many presents can Santa fit in an empty sack?

Just one. After that, it's not empty!

Why couldn't the teacher couldn't find anyone to help her with her gifts?

No one was present.

7.

Elf Jokes

Why did the elf get in trouble at the toy factory?

Because he had a "short" temper!

Why did the elf bring a ladder to school?

Because he wanted to go to high school!

What do you call a greedy elf?

Elfish

What do you get if you cross an elf with a detective?

"Elf"-in trouble!

What did one elf say to the other when they broke a toy?

"We can always fix it with elf tape!"

How do elves greet each other?

"Small world, isn't it?"

Why did the elf go to Santa's workshop party?

To mix and "mingle" with the other elves!

What do you call an elf who tells jokes?

A "knee-slapper"!

Why did the elf put his bed in the fireplace?

He wanted to sleep like a log!

Why did the elf bring a pencil to the toy factory?

To draw up some plans!

How do elves get around?

By riding an "elf"-ephant!

Why did the elf bring a suitcase to the North Pole?

He heard it was a great place to "ice"-olate!

What do you call an elf who loves to eat spicy food?

A "chili" elf!

Why did the elf always carry a pencil behind its ear?

For "elf"--defense!

How do elves stay in shape during the holidays?

They do "elf"-ercises and "jingle" bell workouts!

KNOCK KNOCK

Knock, knock!
Who's there?

Pudding. Pudding who?
Pudding up the Christmas lights!

Knock, knock!
Who's there?

Coal. Coal who?
Coal me when you hear Santa.

Knock, knock!
Who's there?

Luke. Luke who?
Luke at all those presents!

Knock, knock!
Who's there?

Alaska. Alaska who?
Alaska again.
What do you want for Christmas?

Knock, knock!
Who's there?

Snow. Snow who?
Snow time to waste. It's almost Christmas!

Knock, knock!
Who's there?

Harry. Harry who?
Harry up and open your gift!

Knock, knock!
Who's there?

Norway. Norway who?
Norway am I kissing anyone
under the mistletoe!

Knock, knock!
Who's there?

Tank. Tank who?
Tank you for my Christmas present!

Knock, knock!
Who's there?

Kanye. Kanye who?
Kanye help me untangle my Christmas lights?

Knock, knock!
Who's there?

Irish. Irish who?
Irish you a Merry Christmas!

Made in the USA
Las Vegas, NV
20 November 2023

81218923R00046